TIME TO COMPARE!

Which IS DIFFERENT?

T0009813

BY JAGGER YOUSSEF

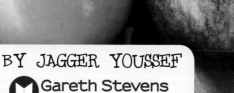
Gareth Stevens
PUBLISHING

first concepts

We can compare!
The circle is different.

3

The baseball
is different.

4

5

The orange
is different.

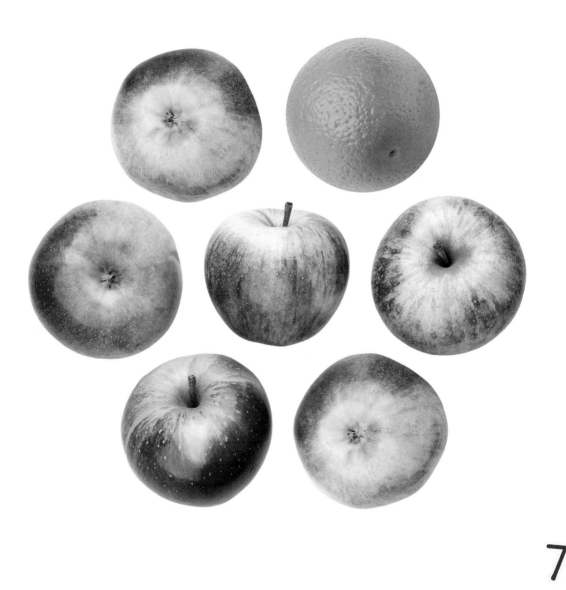

7

The dinosaur
is different.

9

The lemon is different.

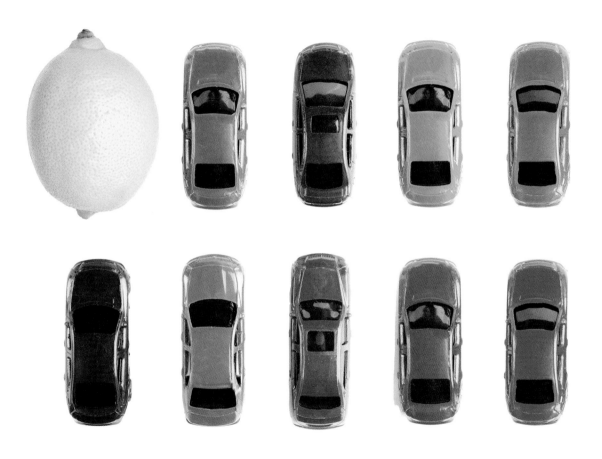

The cat is different.

13

The red balloon
is different.

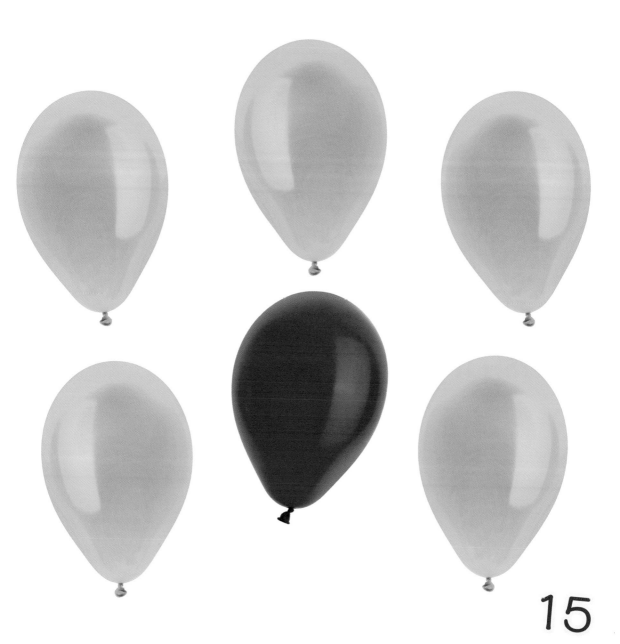

15

The yellow flower
is different.

17

The blue ball
is different.

19

The baby elephant is different.

Point to the
different bike.

23

Please visit our website, www.garethstevens.com. For a free color catalog of all our high-quality books, call toll free 1-800-542-2595 or fax 1-877-542-2596.

Library of Congress Cataloging-in-Publication Data
Names: Youssef, Jagger, author.
Title: Which is different? / Jagger Youssef.
Description: New York : Gareth Stevens Publishing, [2021] | Series: Time to compare! | Includes index.
Identifiers: LCCN 2019043395 | ISBN 9781538255124 (library binding) | ISBN 9781538255100 (paperback) | ISBN 9781538255117 (6 pack)| ISBN 9781538255131 (ebook)
Subjects: LCSH: Comparison (Psychology) in children–Juvenile literature. | Similarity judgment–Juvenile literature.
Classification: LCC BF723.C58 Y68 2021 | DDC 153.7–dc23
LC record available at https://lccn.loc.gov/2019043395

First Edition

Published in 2021 by
Gareth Stevens Publishing
111 East 14th Street, Suite 349
New York, NY 10003

Designer: Sarah Liddell
Editor: Therese Shea

Photo credits: Cover, p. 1 (main) Rinelle/Shutterstock.com; cover, p. 1 (background) oksanka007/Shutterstock.com; pp. 3 (squares), 5 (baseball) Chones/Shutterstock.com; p. 3 (circle) P-fotography/Shutterstock.com; p. 5 (footballs) Carlos E. Santa Maria/Shutterstock.com; p. 7 (apples) bergamont/Shutterstock.com; p. 7 (orange) MaskaRad/Shutterstock.com; p. 9 (bears) Valentin Valkov/Shutterstock.com; p. 9 (dinosaur) aquariagirl1970/Shutterstock.com; p. 11 (lemon) Ian 2010/Shutterstock.com; p. 11 (cars) Love the wind/Shutterstock.com; p. 13 (dogs) Dora Zett/Shutterstock.com; p. 13 (cat) Utekhina Anna/Shutterstock.com; p. 15 Aleksey Patsyuk/Shutterstock.com; p. 17 tr3gin/Shutterstock.com; p. 19 Irina Rogova/Shutterstock.com; p. 21 (adult elephants) Independent birds/Shutterstock.com; p. 21 (baby elephant) Andre Klopper/Shutterstock.com; p. 23 (bicycles) Gena73/Shutterstock.com; p. 23 (tricycle) Boris Medvedev/Shutterstock.com.

Printed in the United States of America

Some of the images in this book illustrate individuals who are models. The depictions do not imply actual situations or events.

CPSIA compliance information: Batch #CS20GS: For further information contact Gareth Stevens, New York, New York at 1-800-542-2595.

Find us on